Marmaduke SUPER DOG

by Brad Anderson

Andrews and McMeel, Inc.
A Universal Press Syndicate Company

Kansas City • New York

ISBN: 0-8362-1212-6
Library of Congress Catalog Card Number: 83-71757

"Life isn't 'dog eat dog,' it's
'dog eat dogfood'!"

"Stop pretending you don't hear me!
I KNOW you do!"

"Go ahead...hit me!"

"What is this...your night to cuddle?"

"You're needed in left field...we're getting murdered!"

"Looks as if Phil changed his dog food again!"

"Give it back! It's MINE!"

"Must you say hello to *all* the girls?"

"He wants me to take him jogging!"

"Pray all you want...you're not getting
into that bed tonight!"

"She did NOT wink at him!"

"It's all right, Marmaduke...my windshield doesn't need cleaning!"

"YOU tell him he has to buy one burger to get one free with that coupon!"

"He's having an identity crisis. He just found out he's a dog and he thought he was people!"

"How is obedience training going?"

"Okay, turn the cat loose."

"I want my chair, newspaper, pipe,
and anything else of mine you have!"

"I wasn't yelling at YOU!"

"Can't you be my SECRET Valentine?"

"Any dogs?"

"A man's best friend doesn't take
his chair away from him!"

"When I got up and went to the bathroom,
Marmaduke stole my warm spot!"

"You're not going to school, and
besides, that's not a lunchbox!"

"Are you just babysitting, or did
she give you custody?"

"An ordinary leash won't do...I need something that will withstand the pull of a diesel locomotive!"

"What do you mean...things could be worse? I just saw him swallow the key!"

"I know you don't want the children to
go back to school, but you'll have
to give me those lunch boxes."

"He takes an interest in every repair job
we have done around here."

"Why can't Marmaduke ever have
a slight injury?"

"That's gotta be the world's biggest
bubble. I gave Marmaduke sixteen
packs of bubble gum!"

"We'd like to use Marmaduke for a while
if you don't need him."

"Most visitors bring him goodies."

"Visiting hours are over."

"I know my feet smell good. I just put bath powder on them!"

"It's a dogcatcher snowman. Now Marmaduke won't be visiting us so often!"

"You wouldn't want him to go out in that snowstorm NAKED, would you?"

"Now I know why Billy's never
late to school!"

"Oh, no you don't! I'm not going to frost
your nose just so you can lick it off!"

"I had no idea Earth had such a hot, wet, forbidding, hostile environment!"

"I really didn't think it would happen this soon!"

"That's the last time I take
you through a car wash!"

"I think I found the rubber ball he was
bouncing around the kitchen!"

"Next, he'll want a uniform!"

"Marmaduke, you can follow Phil around today...I'm leaving him in charge."

"I can always tell when the
Winslows are away!"

"Now he's talking in his sleep!"

"He's been upset all day. You didn't tell him goodbye this morning!"

"That's the ticket, Marmaduke! Revive his will to live!"

"Thanks for keeping me company, Marmaduke!"

"Don't just sit there yawning...get rid of him before he sells me something!"

"We can't walk along streets, avenues and boulevards...WE have to take the vacant lots, junkyards and garbage dumps!"

"You'll have to forgive him. He thinks of that sofa as his."

"Oh, oh! We forgot to guard the eggnog!"

"Mama is paying me to dust the furniture,
but I've found all you have to do
is keep Marmaduke happy!"

"Tear yourself away from your football game long enough to look at this instant replay!"

"They keep ripping it off each other's house!"

"Get your foot off the brake! We're going
to the vet for your shot and that's THAT!"

"That's not the pipe I sent you for!"

"I thought I heard a muffled cry for help coming from somewhere!"

"But, Mama, there's no other place for our feet when Marmaduke sits back here!"

"Oh, no...not ANOTHER big snow!"

"He wants you to hide it and he'll find it...it's LOTS of fun!"

"I suppose YOU want a goodbye kiss, too!"

"I always like the part where Marmaduke
slams on the brakes!"

"Phil, do you realize how long it's been since I've ridden in the front seat?"

"My red shooter is missing!"

"Looks like he's led another break
down at the dog pound."

"Hold it! There's a limit to togetherness!"

"Will I have to pay him anything
to get it back?"

"Why is it you're the only one who
hears my call to dinner?"

"Marmaduke just said 'good morning' to the substitute mailman!"

"I wish he'd stop bringing them home when he can't get the lids off!"

"He's very jealous!"

"Next thing you know he'll want me to build
a guest room onto his doghouse!"

"No, why would I eat a whole jar
of pickled herring?"

"Has anyone seen my bubble pipe?"

"Get your paw off the scale...I'm not giving you MY dessert tonight!"

"How'd you know he's an only dog?"

"After this, don't chase your ball when it rolls under the car!"

"Does this model come with optional heavy-duty springs?"

"It's too bad you woke Marmaduke with your vacuum cleaner...he's getting even with it!"

"He loves to go fishing."

"Don't worry...the mother bird won't let the babies fly until they're ready!"

"Must you always have the last bark?"

"Guess where we'll start this year's
spring cleaning?"

"Our energy crisis is whenever he has
too much of it!"

"Mom, bang the refrigerator door...I can't get Marmaduke out of the cockpit!"

"He likes to be part of the conversation."

"If he starts to huff and puff, open
the door and let him in!"

"Hold it! I'M the one who
declares snack time!"

"Whatever you want to do at 4 a.m., you're doing alone!"

"You timed it perfectly. I just sat down!"

"We just never told him he's supposed
to hate cats!"

"We...and that includes YOU...are on
an austerity budget!"

"I think the magic key is...pound on the door with a bone!"

"Mama, Marmaduke wants to wash his pet frog off..."

"I wish you hadn't told Marmaduke the price of dog food went up again!"

"What is it you're trying to tell me now, Marmaduke?"

"Grab his paws so he can't blast away on the horn...we're passing his girlfriend's house!"

"Where is Marmaduke? It's time for his pill!"

"OK, OK, take the chair!"

"Marmaduke is trying to help us save
gas...we've got a tailwind behind us now!"

"He never met a garbage can
he didn't like!"

"All right, all right! Never again!"

"Goodness! Whatever has the newspaper printed about dogs now?"

"When do we stop playing 'baby'? This is his 16th bottle!"

"After this, wait until he's out of his dog-house before you tell him to roll over!"

"I really can't say I'm enjoying this cookout!"

"You did, too, drink my root beer. I can hear it fizzing in your stomach!"

"Marmaduke's having trouble convincing Snyder that he loves him."

"The city dump wants you to put everything back in one big heap again!"

"He was supposed to baby-sit for a few minutes, but the mother's been gone all day!"

"I can't find my contoured pillow and I just *can't* muss up my hair tonight!"

"This nose feels familiar!"

"But I don't want to play tug-of-war
right now!"

"He was watching me dunk my cookie, and
all of a sudden..."

"No, no! There's not room for you to play in the water, too!"

"So you're not pedigreed! My ancestors didn't come over on the Mayflower, either!"

"Nothing can hold Marmaduke when the ice cream truck comes by!"

"Whenever I can't find something, I always check Marmaduke's stockpile!"

"Someone else is calling about missing a trash can!"

"When did he get this notion that he's a hood ornament?"

"Take the number and I'll call back later...if I leave now I'll never get my chair back!"

"Thank you for being a dependable watchdog...but I'm tired of being watched!"

"Just once I wish we could sneak off
without him!"

"If I put you out you want to look in, and if I
leave you in you want to look out!"

"Thanks for fetching part of the paper!"

"You must be carrying mints in your purse!"

"Stop backing up...that vacuum cleaner
you hear is clear over at Snyder's house!"

"Watch how far Pop throws the beach ball
when Marmaduke puts his cold nose
in his back!"

"Hey! It's your turn to PUSH!"

"I hate when he's dreaming...now he's
scratching my ear!"

"Thanks for wanting to carry my umbrella...but I have a small request!"

"I can understand the jogging craze... but HOPPING?"

"Come back, Marmaduke! You're sicker than you realize!"

"I see ONE tennis player didn't bother to phone me about his complaint!"

"I found two gray hairs and
you're to blame!"

"On a lovely summer day you have
me wishing all this was covered
by a winter snow!"

"Marmaduke, we sell it by the glass, not the pitcher!"

"Move over, Marmaduke...our air conditioner is on the fritz."

"You shouldn't have said, 'Let's flip for the chair!'"

"Well, next time you decide to knock over a beehive, you'd better run faster!"

"Do you realize that's his fourth
romance this week?!"

"The part I dread is his
good morning slurp!"

"What have you done this time?"

"I tried to tell him it was a phony, but he insisted on sampling it!"

"Stop rapping your dish on the fence!
I know you're there!"

"Honestly, Phil...stop panting!"

"Tell the truth, Billy! Does Marmaduke really eat Chihuahuas for breakfast?"

"Well, you've got hairy legs too, you know!"

"Ever get the feeling you're being watched?"

"Phil! It's ten minutes past jogging time!"

"With a peephole, no less!"

"That ice cream vendor seems to
be tailgating us!"

"His night light needs new batteries!"

"He's fine, so until he tires of playing dead, enjoy the peace and quiet!"

"After breaking a lamp, knocking over the mailman and eating our lunch, don't give me that 'Why am I being punished?' look!"

"Forget about guarding the club treasury,
Marmaduke...nobody paid his dues!"

"No, I don't want to trade my popcorn
for your dog biscuits!"

"Dottie! Help me up! I have an eight o'clock appointment with him at the vet!"

"Let's get a different bad guy...Marmaduke is too fast for us to cut off at the pass!"

"He's the only dog I know with
jogging headphones!"

"Do you realize that tonight the owners of
four French poodles called here?"

"Sure, sure! I'll ask the company to
make a liver flavor!"

"Marmaduke WOOFED just as the
stopped up drain PLOOFED and
Mr. Snyder blew his top!"

"Sometimes I swear he's 99% dog food!"

"Dottie...someone to see you!"

"When Marmaduke doesn't want to move...he usually doesn't!"

"Sure he can do tricks. He can make a ten-pound bag of dog food disappear just like that!"

"Well, hello there. My, you've stayed awake
a long time this morning!"

"Why don't you go watch Phil shave?"

"From the way your tail is wagging, I don't think you're listening!"

"The Winslow kids must be coming!"

"Whatever you're buttering me up for,
the answer is 'NO'!"

"Easy, Marmaduke, easy!
I'm just learning!"

"Will you come down if Daddy gives you
a package of wieners?"

"I like a car with good pickup!"

"You'd better stop...If Marmaduke is late for school again, you're in trouble!"

"You take the couch and I'll take the doghouse!"

"A salesman disturbed Marmaduke's nap!"

"HE may be asleep, but his stomach sure isn't!"

"Where's the breath freshener? He had
garlic last night!"

"My shoes, my shoes...did you bring
me my shoes?"

"When will I be big enough to get to the school bus on my own?"

"Put another quarter in the meter...I don't want to be the one who tickets him."

"Look at this news story...'The Case
of the Missing Dogcatcher'!"

"I've got to break him of these
flying leaps onto my lap!"

"Here, Pop, hold this a minute..."

"The air is thick with mischief-plotting...separate corners."

"He has two speeds...fast and
full speed ahead!"

"If you can't find your toothbrush,
Marmaduke will loan you his."

"Tell <u>him</u> dinner is ready!"

"Skip his snacks?...You tell him, Doctor!"

"No, you can't come in! I just mopped the floor!"

"Your timing is way off!"

"Marmaduke liked school so much that we couldn't get him out of the cafeteria!"

"I'll think of a charge...licking a traffic cop's face HAS to be illegal!"

"We're testing his wardrobe in case we have an early winter."

"I see 'Ace Brooms, Brushes and Bristles' are on the upswing."

"Breakfast in my bed is bad enough, but when did he learn to do that?"

"Any chance of your letting me up?"

"I wish I hadn't taken you to that
frog-jumping contest!"

"I'll have to hang up now, Helen. It looks
like it's time to get dinner started!"